Agnese Baruzzi

Find Me !

Adventures in the Forest

Play along to
sharpen your vision
and mind

A WOLF WHO WASN'T SCARY!

There are many animals in the forest: moles, squirrels, rabbits, wild boars, porcupines, foxes, and lots of birds. All of them fear the gray wolves. The wolves have sharp teeth, killer claws, great speed, and huge appetites! These wolves can spot and chase down prey in a flash. All, that is, except one: Bernard.

Bernard is not a ferocious wolf. He is not fast. Even worse, he can't see very well.
To see anything at all, he has to wear his big, thick glasses.

Bernard was sad. If only he could be a tiny bit frightening!
But in his big glasses, he thought he looked funny
and not fierce. Whoever heard of a wolf in glasses?
So Bernard did not wear them.

Bernard's friend Michael the squirrel did not mind that his
friend was not fierce. (In fact, he liked it that way!)
One day when Bernard started to cry,
Michael decided he would help.

"You're so lucky that you have those glasses," Michael told Bernard. "When you wear them, you can learn to see better than anyone in the forest. You just need to practice."

"Sharpen your eyes and try to find me!"

"But how?" Bernard asked.

"I'll show you!" the squirrel said. "Wear your glasses and then I'll hide in lots of hard-to-find places, and you have to find me. We'll explore the forest from top to bottom, meet all the animals living there, splash around in the pond, and look up at the sky. I'll hide behind trees, in hollows, under dried leaves, or tucked under the wings of a bird. Your job is to find me wherever I am!"

"And that's not all. I'm going to give you some tests. There will be special questions, and you'll need your eagle-eyed powers of observation to get them right."

"By the end of our adventure, you'll feel proud to wear your glasses. And the other wolves will respect your awesome eyesight!"

"Ready, steady, go!"

One porcupine has curly spines. Can you find him?

Where is his brush?

Who is having a nap?

Three toy animals are hiding among the porcupines. Can you find them?

Who sleeps all day?

Who has been sneaking blackberries?

Who was just born?

You need these four ingredients for the eagle-eye potion. They're all hidden in the forest. Can you find them?

Who is scared to get dirty?

Who is angry because he wasn't invited?

Who is playing hide and seek?

There is a picnic in the forest, and six animals are on their way to eat the watermelon. Who are they?

All of these animals can fly except for one. Can you find it?

Find the pairs!
Each deer on the left page
has an identical
twin on the right page.

Freddy

Freddy the boar has lost his twin. Only one of the wild boars below is identical to him. Where is he?

Who is different from all the others? Only one snake does not have a twin. Which one?

Who has one eye shut?

Who is trying to hypnotize you?

Who looks hungry?

Find the pairs! Each owl on the left page has a twin on the right page. Can you match them?

Who was just born?

Who is sleepy?

Who is having a snack?

Can you spot the secret passage?

Find my food for the winter!

Can you see a mysterious bone?

Three animals have left tracks in the forest. Can you spot them? Who do the tracks belong to?

Acorns and pine cones grow in the forest, and squirrels love to eat them. Can you spot the three foods in the picture that don't grow on trees?

Which mushroom is different from all the others?

Which mushrooms are poisonous?

Which mushroom has a bite out of it?

Ten snails are hiding
among the mushrooms.
Can you find them?

Lots of frogs live in the pond. There's another animal hiding here, too. Who is it?

Who is having a good cry?

Who has a sore throat?

Who is laughing a lot?

Who is disguised as a king?

Who is singing a happy song?

Who is building a nest?

Find the pairs!
All the birds on the left page have an identical twin on the right page.

Can you spot a colander?

Can you find a tasty snack?

And a hat?

Tortoises and snails are not known for their speed. But hiding among them is a much faster animal. Can you find it?

Can you see a sweet treat?

Which two things look
like butterflies but aren't?

Where is the kite?

Which butterfly is not like all the others? Only one is different. Can you find it?

The forest animals have invited three friends who live far away. Can you spot them and their suitcases?

Did you answer all the
questions?

FIND OUT HERE!

You'll find the answers to all the games on the next few pages. Check your powers of observation and decide if you need to go back and repeat the exercise! You'll notice that some solutions have:

★ A star to indicate the main characters in the game and in the special questions.

④ Numbers to help you check if you have found all the animal pairs.

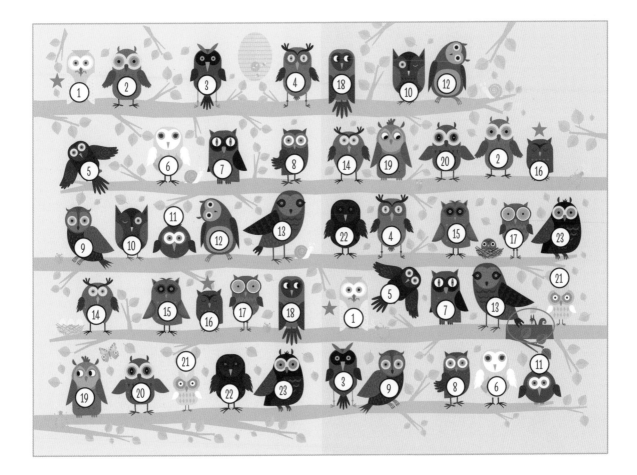

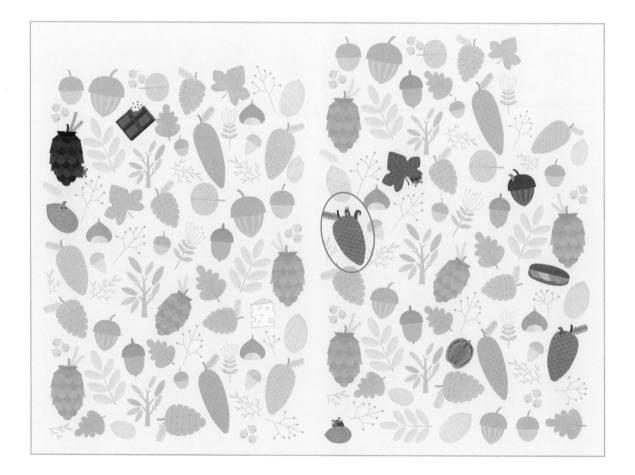

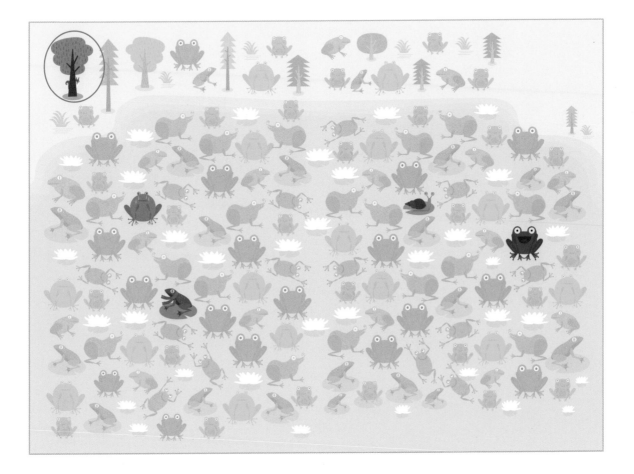

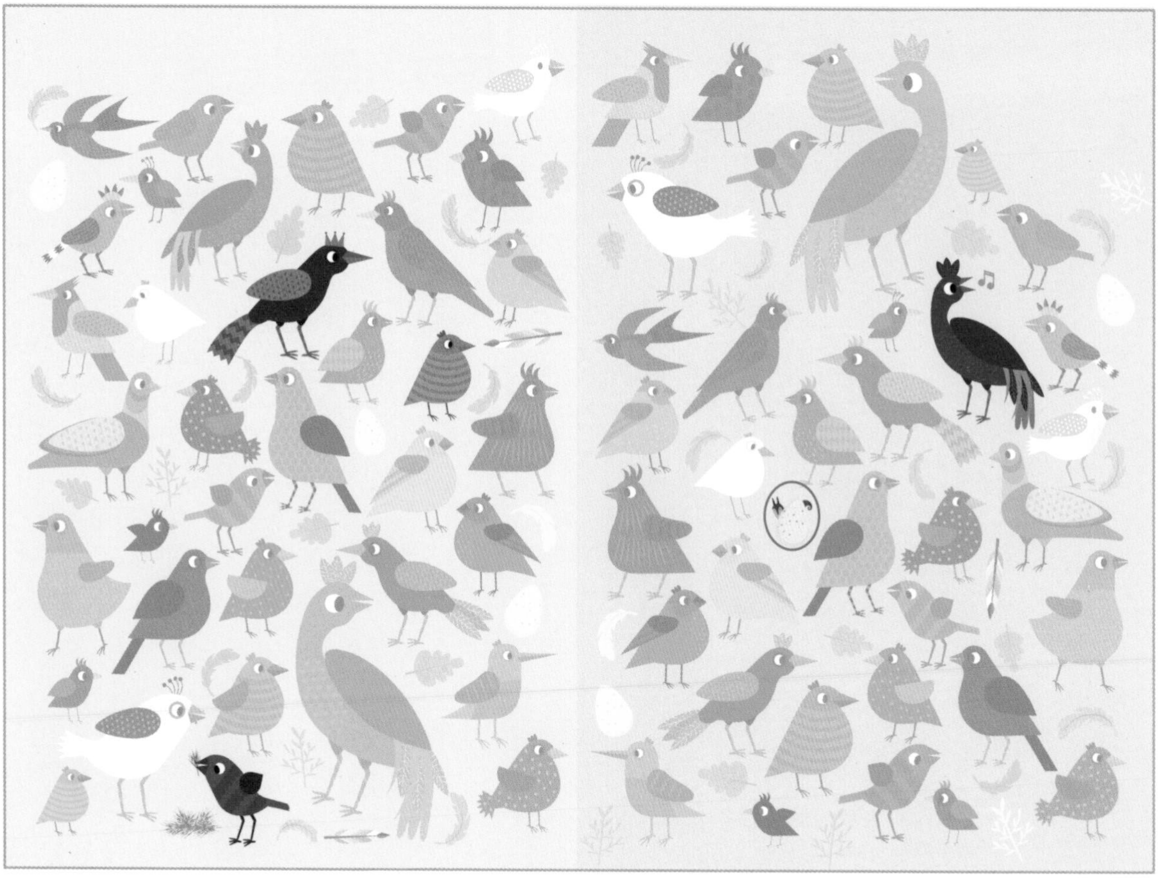

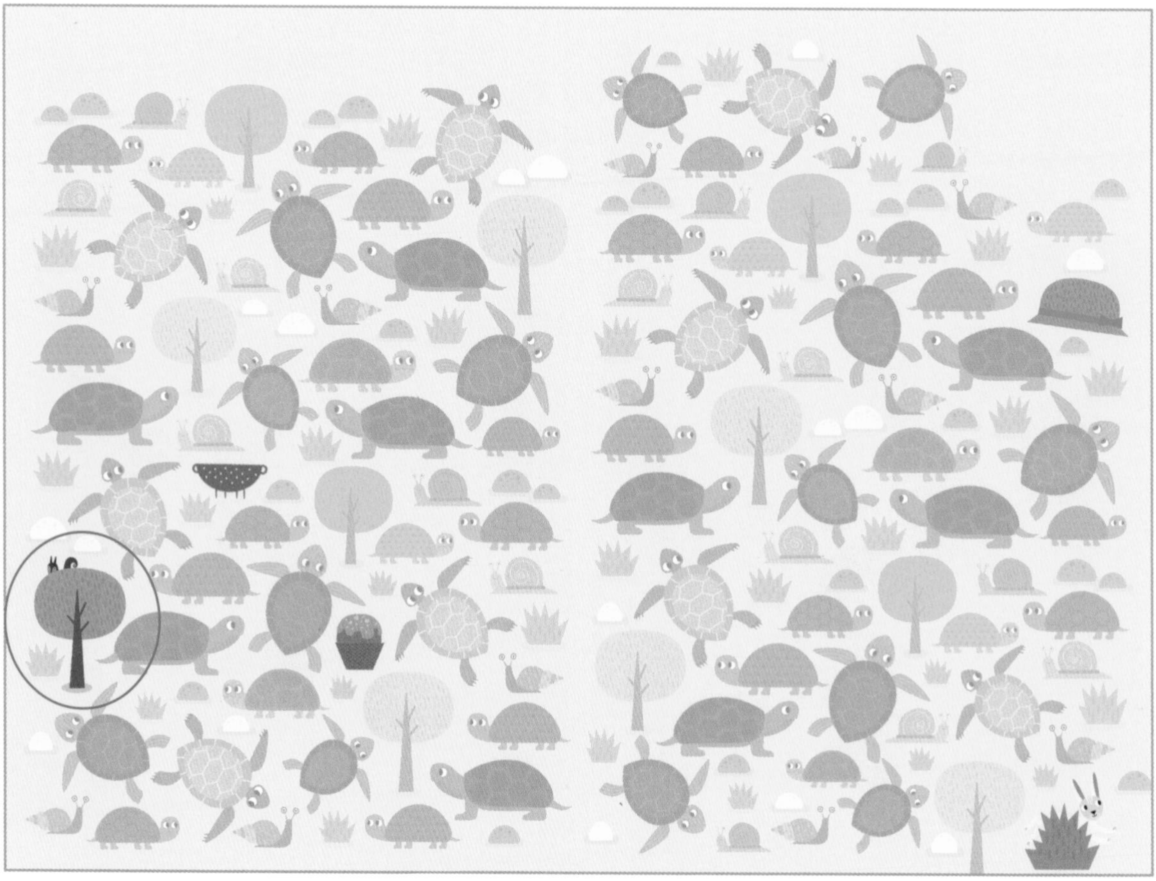

Agnese Baruzzi

Born in 1980, Agnese has a degree in graphic design from the High Institute for Artistic Industries (ISIA) in Urbino, Italy. Since 2011, she has been working as an illustrator and author for kids' books in Italy, the United Kingdom, Japan, Portugal, the United States, France, and South Korea. She organizes workshops for kids and adults in schools and libraries, as well as collaborates with agencies, graphic design studios, and publishers. In the last few years Agnese has illustrated several books for White Star Kids.

White Star Kids® is a registered trademark property of White Star s.r.l.

© 2019 White Star s.r.l.
Piazzale Luigi Cadorna, 6
20123 Milan, Italy
www.whitestar.it

Translation: Denise Muir

Originally published in 2019 as *Find Me! Adventures in the Forest with Bernard the Wolf* by White Star, this North American version titled *Find Me! Adventures in the Forest* is published in 2020 by Fox Chapel Publishing Company, Inc. Reproduction of its contents is strictly prohibited without written permission from the rights holder.

Happy Fox Books is an imprint of Fox Chapel Publishing Company, Inc., 903 Square Street, Mount Joy, PA 17552.

ISBN 978-1-64124-047-5 (Hardcover)
ISBN 978-1-64124-101-4 (Paperback)

Library of Congress Control Number: 2019955450

To learn more about the other great books from Fox Chapel Publishing, or to find a retailer near you, call toll-free 800-457-9112 or visit us at *www.FoxChapelPublishing.com*.

We are always looking for talented authors. To submit an idea, please send a brief inquiry to acquisitions@foxchapelpublishing.com.

Fox Chapel Publishing makes every effort to use environmentally friendly paper for printing.

Printed in China